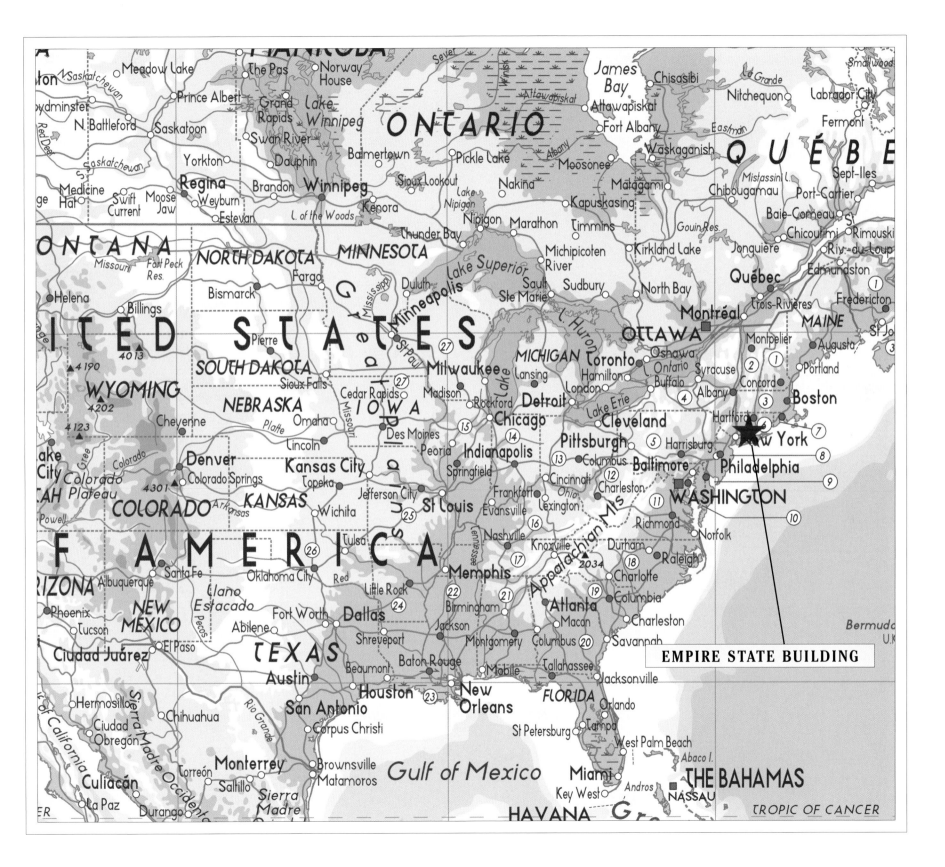

EMPIRE STATE BUILDING

Published by Creative Education
123 South Broad Street
Mankato, Minnesota 56001

Creative Education is an imprint of The Creative Company.

Designed by Stephanie Blumenthal
Production design by Melinda Belter
Art direction by Rita Marshall

Photographs by Alamy (1Apix, Ambient Images Inc., Arcaid, Atmosphere Picture Library, Black Star, Comstock Images, wendy connett, Dory, Dennis Hallinan, Henry Westheim Photography, ImageState, Jon Arnold Images, Lebrecht Music and Arts Photo Library, J Marshall – Tribaleye, Michele Molinari, PCL, Chuck Pefley, Pier Photography, Robert Harding Picture Library Ltd, Frances M. Roberts, Scenics & Science, Alex Segre, Dean Shults, Peter Steiner, Max Stuart, John Taylor, Visions of America, LLC, Jim West, Reven T.C. Wurman), Design Maps, Inc., Getty Images (Mitchell Funk, Lewis W. Hine / George Eastman House, RKO Radio Pictures, Pete Seaward)

Printed in the United States of America

Library of Congress Cataloging-in-Publication Data
Peterson, Sheryl.
Empire State Building / by Sheryl Peterson.
p. cm. — (Modern wonders of the world)
Includes index.
ISBN-13: 978-1-58341-439-2
1. Empire State Building (New York, N.Y.)—Juvenile literature. 2. New York (N.Y.)—Buildings, structures, etc.—
Juvenile literature. I. Title. II. Series.

F128.8.E46P48 2005   974.7'1—dc22   2005050658

First edition

2 4 6 8 9 7 5 3 1

EMPIRE STATE BUILDING

AUTHOR
Sheryl Peterson

MODERN WONDERS
OF THE WORLD

CREATIVE EDUCATION

The Empire State Building, renowned for both its height and its beauty, is visible from nearly every point in New York City—as well as from points well outside the city.

High above the New York City skyline, like a giant rocket ready to blast into space, towers the majestic Empire State Building. This soaring **skyscraper**, built during the **Great Depression**, was the victor in a contest to construct the tallest building in America and quickly became the emblem of New York and a prominent example of American inventiveness. With its sleek **Art Deco** architecture, the limestone and **steel** structure rises regally above noisy streets filled with bustling shoppers, honking yellow taxicabs, and fluttering pigeons. Although the awe-inspiring landmark has since been surpassed in height by several other skyscrapers created around the globe, it remains one of architecture's crown jewels, as well as one of the world's most famous attractions.

4

A RACE TO THE SKY

The Flatiron Building (below) and the Singer Building (right) were early New York City skyscrapers.

In the 1920s, the limits of height were rapidly changing in the world of architecture. With the invention of elevators, central heating systems, the telephone, and light yet strong steel supports that replaced old-fashioned iron ones, skyscrapers came to dominate the American skyline at the turn of the 20th century. Chicago had been the first city to earn a reputation as a skyscraper center with the completion of its 10-story Home Insurance Building in 1885.

New York City had 188 buildings of 21 stories or more by 1929, including the 55-story Woolworth Building, but bigger buildings were needed. Hundreds of immigrants

were arriving monthly in the overcrowded metropolis, and land was scarce. If business and apartment buildings couldn't spread out, they had to go up.

In this era of exciting change, several multi-millionaires chose to use their wealth in extravagant ways beyond fancy cars and lavish homes. A fierce competition developed among the very rich to build the highest skyscraper in New York City. Building the tallest structure would bring recognition to the owners, glory to New York, and high office rents from business tenants.

During this huge construction boom, two men—neither with any background in archi-

6

The Woolworth Building was commissioned by Frank W. Woolworth, the wealthy owner of a chain of "five-and-dime" stores. After its completion in 1913, the intricate skyscraper stood as the tallest building in the world for 17 years.

The stock market experienced a tremendous boom during the 1920s, with stock prices increasing rapidly, but on "Black Tuesday," stock tickers (below) reported sharply falling prices. Many people, including those in luxurious Manhattan townhouses (right), soon found themselves jobless and broke.

tecture or construction—came together to plan the skyscraper that would become known as the Empire State Building: Alfred E. Smith, a former New York governor, and his friend John J. Raskob, vice president of the General Motors automobile company. The outgoing Smith, recognized by his Derby hat, became the enterprise's spokesperson, while Raskob put up most of the money needed and convinced other wealthy friends to invest in the project.

Smith and Raskob named their planned building after New York state's nickname, "The Empire State." They hired William Lamb, an architect at the firm Shreve,

Lamb, and Harmon, to design the Empire State Building. Basing his design on a simple pencil, Lamb drew the clean, soaring lines that would become the amazing skyscraper. The new building would be built in the hub of New York City, provide easily accessible office space, and, of course, be taller than any other structure.

Before construction could begin, the once hugely popular Waldorf Astoria Hotel in the **borough** of Manhattan needed to be leveled to make room for the new structure. The day demolition began, Tuesday, October 1, 1929, turned out to be an unlucky day for all Americans. "Black Tuesday" was the day the **stock market** crashed. Businesses became worthless

8

By the 1920s, more than two million people lived in the island borough of Manhattan, connected to the rest of New York City by beautiful bridges such as the Manhattan Bridge. Today, the Manhattan Bridge is still well-traveled, and from the right angle, its tower creates a picturesque frame for the Empire State Building.

Lewis Hine, a native of Wisconsin, photographed workers in precarious positions as they secured the framework of the Empire State Building in 1930. Strapped into a safety belt with camera in hand, Hine bravely swung out in a specially designed basket some 1,000 feet (305 m) above 5th Avenue.

overnight, and thousands of people were suddenly unemployed. It was the beginning of the Great Depression. Banks closed, and people across the nation lost all of their savings.

During the Great Depression, many building projects were halted due to lack of money. Fortunately, construction of Smith and Raskob's skyscraper was able to go forward. The scarcity of jobs created eager workers, and Smith and Raskob paid good wages. For months, trucks loaded with the rubble that had been the Waldorf Astoria Hotel left the site. Barges hauled debris down the East River and dumped it in the Atlantic Ocean 20 miles (32 km) out at sea.

During this time, another massive skyscraper on 42nd Street in New York City was rapidly nearing completion. Smith and Raskob watched as the elegant Chrysler Building took shape and climbed to 925 feet (283 m). The two men then boldly announced that their building would be 1,000 feet (305 m) tall. Car manufacturing millionaire Walter Chrysler added a thin, stainless steel tower to the top of his skyscraper to make it 1,048 feet (319 m) tall, but Smith and Raskob countered by altering their plan to include five more stories and a scenic observatory. They were determined not to lose the skyscraper race!

As the owners of the Chrysler Building (far left) and the Empire State Building (left) battled to build the tallest skyscraper in the world, construction workers on the two projects found themselves suspended above New York City streets at record heights.

MANHATTAN'S MASTERPIECE

The Empire State Building is struck by lightning about 100 times a year. Since lightning strikes the tallest object available, the tower serves as a protective **lightning rod** for the surrounding area. The building's steel framework helps to direct the electricity from lightning strikes harmlessly into the ground.

With the Waldorf Astoria Hotel cleared away, excavation for the Empire State Building project began on January 22, 1930, at the junction of 5th Avenue and 34th Street, within walking distance of New York's famous Times Square and Broadway. On March 17, St. Patrick's Day, the construction company of Starrett Brothers and Eken began placing steel **columns** on concrete **piers** anchored solidly into the bedrock below.

Next, workers attached steel **beams** horizontally to the columns, forming a 3-D grid throughout the structure that gave it strength. The building's skeleton rose at the amazing rate of four and a half floors per week. To save construction time, materials were loaded onto miniature railroad cars and pushed by hand to workers in need of supplies. As the floors rose, the railroad was taken apart and reassembled higher up. Concrete was poured for the building's floors to protect against fires.

At dizzying heights, steelworkers performed unbelievable acts of skill and daring to position and **rivet** the beams of the building. New York residents honked horns and craned their necks to marvel at the acrobatic work as the steelworkers climbed and swung like spiders hundreds of feet in the air. Construction progressed at a startlingly rapid pace, largely because workers were in dire need of money and worked seven days a week, including holidays.

As was the case during its construction, the Empire State Building today bustles with activity seven days a week, every day of the year. Lights glow from row upon row of windows at all hours of the night.

The needle-nosed tower that is the Empire State Building's 87th to 102nd floors was originally built as a **dirigible** mooring mast. It was planned that huge airships would hook up to the mast and send passengers down, but the idea was deemed too dangerous and scrapped. Today, the top portion of the building is used for television broadcasting.

The Empire State Building's first five stories rose straight up, covering an area of 83,890 square feet (7,550 sq m). Starting on the sixth floor, **setbacks** were created to gently slope the tower's higher floors, making the building appear even taller. The setbacks allowed sunlight to shine and air to circulate down to the surrounding streets. Red-framed windows, 6,500 in all, dotted the building's exterior, ensuring office workers a view and a breeze—important since there was no air-conditioning. Seventy-three fast-paced elevators were installed to whisk people to the top of the building and back down in a hurry.

William Lamb and his associate architects wanted the outer **façade** of the building to make a grand impression. Skyscrapers of the 1800s and early 1900s generally resembled plain boxes with simple stone and glass walls, but the Art Deco movement of the 1920s saw buildings as true works of art. The Empire State Building's architects created a modernistic design that used pale Indiana limestone and granite on the exterior, topped with smooth steel strips and shiny aluminum panels to conceal the rough stone edges. Beneath the glistening exterior, builders layered bricks for insulation.

Many buildings throughout New York City look out on the Empire State Building and its distinctive tower of glass, steel, and aluminum. On foggy or misty days, the 200-foot-tall (60 m) tower is often impossible to see from the ground.

Many world leaders and celebrities, including Queen Elizabeth of England, Cuban president Fidel Castro, and Brazilian soccer star Pele, have admired the view from the top of the Empire State Building. Photos of famous visitors are on display on the building's concourse level, below the lobby.

The relief image (opposite) in the Empire State Building's lobby greets visitors headed for the building's higher floors.

Flanking the Empire State Building's high entrance door were two stately stone eagles, and red-veined marble imported from France and Italy lined the lobby area. A dazzling metal relief image of the tower, superimposed on a giant map of New York state in the lobby, welcomed future tenants.

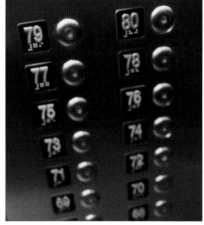

Thanks to the hard work of as many as 3,500 workers at a time, the Empire State Building's construction was finished in only 1 year and 45 days, or about 7 million man hours, a time that remains a record today for buildings of such magnitude. In addition, the building cost of the 102-story skyscraper came to only $24 million, half of the $50 million originally projected. When the last rivet, made of solid gold, was hammered in by former governor Al Smith himself, the Empire State Building was officially the tallest building in the world.

The skyscraper opened on May 1, 1931, when President Herbert Hoover symbolically pressed a button in the White House turning on the lights. Despite the awed reception given the structure, the U.S. was still in the grip of the Depression, and many offices went unrented until the 1940s, earning the building the nickname the "Empty State Building."

A NATIONAL TREASURE

Like neighboring Central Park (right), the Empire State Building has appeared in many movies, including King Kong. *The skyscraper used to share the skyline with the World Trade Center towers (opposite, at right).*

The Empire State Building remained the tallest building in the world for 40 years until New York's World Trade Center towers were built in 1972. Since that time, several other taller buildings, including the Sears Tower in Chicago, have been built. Sadly, the World Trade Center towers collapsed after terrorists crashed airplanes into them on September 11, 2001. The tragedy made the Empire State Building once again the tallest skyscraper in New York City.

Over the years, the Empire State Building has made head-

lines in many ways. On July 28, 1945, at the end of World War II, a B-25 bomber accidentally crashed into the north side of the building in dense fog. One of the plane's engines tore through the office walls and came out the south side. Fourteen people were killed in the accident, but amazingly, the building suffered no major structural damage.

The Empire State Building's imposing form has been featured in more than 100 movies. The first and most popular was *King Kong*, released in 1933. In the movie, the main character, a giant ape captured from a mysterious island, climbs to the top of the building holding actress Fay Wray in his hand. After fighting

In 1983, in honor of the 50th anniversary of the film *King Kong*, an inflatable, 85-foot (26 m) ape was placed atop the Empire State Building. However, strong winds soon tore a huge hole in Kong, and he toppled, deflated.

A penny tossed off the Empire State Building never hits the ground. Because of the wind effect on the skyscraper, falling objects are pushed against the building. Coins dropped from the 86th floor land harmlessly on the 80th-floor setback and are collected by electricians when they change the building's lights.

off attacking planes, King Kong dies by falling off the skyscraper.

The Empire State Building is famous for lighting up the New York sky. In 1932, a searchlight on the top of the building first announced the election of Franklin D. Roosevelt as U.S. president. New colored lights illuminated the sky in 1976 for America's bicentennial celebration. Today, lights on the building's top 30 floors change regularly for different occasions. At Christmas, they shine red and green, and at Hanukkah, they beam in shades of blue and white. In the spring and fall, during peak bird migration times, the

lights are turned off so birds won't be distracted and fly into the building!

Every year since 1977, the Empire State Building has hosted the Run-Up Race. Men and women from around the world gather to dash up 1,576 steps to the building's 86th-floor observatory. Teams such as the New York City policemen and firefighters challenge each other to win medals and to raise money for charities. On all other days of the year, the stairs are used only for emergencies.

Over the years, a number of alterations have been made to the Empire State Building. A television **antenna** added to the top in 1950

*Whether one peers down
at the busy streets nearly
a quarter-mile (400 m)
below (opposite) or gazes
out over New York City
to the distant horizon, the
view from the Empire
State Building's 86th-floor
observatory is breath-
taking, day or night.*

The height of the Empire State Building leads to interesting comparisons. If the Eiffel Tower in Paris, France, were placed atop the Great Pyramid in Cairo, Egypt, the Empire State Building would still exceed their height by 38 feet (12 m).

Today, Taiwan's Taipei 101 (far right), Malaysia's Petronas Towers (right), and seven other buildings stand taller than the Empire State Building.

raised the total height from 1,250 feet (381 m) to 1,472 feet (449 m) and sharpened the building's lean silhouette. In 1963, a series of colorful stained-glass murals were installed in the 34th street lobby. These panels depict the seven traditional wonders of the world and the Empire State Building as the eighth wonder. In 1981, on the occasion of its Golden Jubilee, or 50th anniversary, the building was designated an official New York City landmark, which means it can never be torn down.

Today, the skyscraper race is far from over. By 2006, proposals had been made to construct dozens of buildings that may break the world record for height currently held by the Taipei 101, a 101-story office building in Taipei, Taiwan. Plans were also in the works for a building that would steal the title of "New York City's Tallest": The Freedom Tower, a 1,776-foot (541 m) skyscraper to be built at the site of the devastated World Trade Center. Still, the Empire State Building stands as bold and beautiful as the day it was first imagined. This elegant, rocket-like structure, reaching up toward the stars, remains an enduring symbol of American dreams.

EMPIRE STATE BUILDING

SEEING THE WONDER

Although navigating the busy streets of New York City can be tricky, the city's extensive public transportation system brings visitors within steps of the Empire State Building's main entrance on 5th Avenue. Once inside the building, all visitors must pass through a security checkpoint before continuing on to the observatory.

Each year, more than three million tourists seek out the Empire State Building. Visitors generally take a taxi or subway train to the building's location on 5th Avenue and 34th street in Manhattan. The landmark is impossible to miss. Entering through the 5th Avenue doors, visitors can view the building's interior architecture and lobby art exhibits or head directly for the elevators.

Two elevators carry tourists up through the business section of the building to the Visitors' Center on the 86th floor. The 86th-floor observatory, with its open decks and glass-enclosed area, is accessible rain or shine from 8:00 A.M. to midnight, with the last elevator

ride up at 11:15 P.M. On a clear day, tourists can gaze for 80 miles (130 km) into New York and the neighboring states of New Jersey, Pennsylvania, Connecticut, and Massachusetts. The observatory is handicap-accessible, and high-powered, coin-operated binoculars give sightseers of all ages a bird's-eye view of the Statue of Liberty, Yankee Stadium, and the lush greenery of nearby Central Park.

As of 2006, admission to the observatory was $15.50 for adults, $14.50 for teens, and $10.50 for children. Visitors can purchase tickets at the Empire State Building or in advance from the building's official Web site (www.esbnyc.com).

2 6

Sometimes during stormy weather, a build-up of atmospheric electricity forms around the Empire State Building's highest points, and "St. Elmo's Fire," a bluish-white static discharge, can be seen glowing outside the observatory fence. This same phenomenon can create electric sparks when people kiss on the observation deck.

In 1994, without any warning, French urban climber Alain "Spiderman" Robert scaled the Empire State Building's exterior from bottom to top. He used no safety devices, only his bare hands and feet clad in slip-on shoes. Robert has also climbed the Eiffel Tower, the Sears Tower, and the Sydney Opera House.

People could once visit the building's 102nd-floor observatory, but that area has been closed to the public since 1998. Long lines caused traffic jams to the larger 86th-floor observatory, and both decks offer almost the same view.

Another popular tourist attraction within the Empire State Building is the New York Skyride, a simulated helicopter ride on the building's second floor. Visitors fly from the Empire State Building, glide past the Statue of Liberty, and zip through Times Square—all from a theater seat. The Skyride is open daily from 10:00 A.M. to 10:00 P.M.

Between the lobby and the observatory, the Empire State Building contains many business establishments, ranging from television studios and radio stations to financial institutions to fashion designers. There are no personal residences in the building. Before leaving, tourists may stop at the building's pizza restaurant or ice-cream parlor. Many others end their visit with a stop at the 86th-floor souvenir shop to purchase scenic postcards, small pewter replicas of the skyscraper, King Kong buttons, or T-shirts proclaiming "I love New York."

Tourists to New York soon discover that no matter what they're doing— riding a ferry on the Hudson River, exiting the subway, or even looking into the glass of another skyscraper—the Empire State Building is never far from their minds.

EMPIRE STATE  BUILDING

Location: New York City (Manhattan), New York

Time of construction: March 1930 to April 1931

Opening date: May 1, 1931: President Herbert Hoover pressed a symbolic button in Washington, D.C., to turn on the building's lights

Composition: Steel, brick, and stone, including limestone, granite, and marble

Architects: William Lamb (principal designer), Richmond Shreve, and Arthur Harmon

Work force involved: ~ 3,500 laborers

Height: 102 stories; 1,472 feet (448 m) to the top of the antenna

Area covered (ground floor): 1.9 acres (.8 ha)

Number of steps: 1,576, from the street level to the 86th floor

Cost to build: $24 million

Funded by: General Motors executive John J. Raskob and other private investors

Tenants: ~ 880 businesses and 25,000 workers

Visitors per year: ~ 3.8 million

GLOSSARY

antenna — a tall metal rod or wire that sends out or receives radio waves

Art Deco — a style of architecture and art popular in the 1920s and '30s characterized by bold, geometric shapes and swirling designs

beams — rods made of steel or wood used for horizontal support in construction

borough — a part, or division, of New York City; New York includes the five boroughs of Manhattan, Brooklyn, Queens, The Bronx, and Staten Island

columns — rods made of steel or wood used for vertical support in construction

dirigible — a balloon-like airship that contains compartments filled with gas and a place for passengers; it is also called a blimp or zeppelin

façade — the face, or front, of a building

Great Depression — a time from 1929 to 1939 when there was widespread unemployment in the U.S. and a major drop-off in the production and sale of goods

lightning rod — a tall metal rod that attracts lightning and safely channels it into the ground to protect a building from damage

piers — concrete supports between a building's columns and the bedrock, or natural rock, underneath the building

rivet — to hammer metal pins or bolts (called rivets) through steel supports to hold the supports together

setbacks — areas of tall buildings that are built back inward at particular heights in order to better allow light and ventilation to reach the street below

skyscraper — a building that is more than 20 stories tall and is supported by a steel frame

steel — metal that is made from iron but is lighter and has five times the strength

stock market — a system of buying and selling stocks, or investments, in a company to make a profit; America's stock market crashed (dropped off suddenly) in 1929, causing the Great Depression

31

INDEX